Fun Secret…

Did you know? The book cover shows the coloring of this dog – only a tiny piece. Which piece is that?

Answer: **əsou əɥʇ**

50 Cool Animal Patterns at Your Finger Tips:

1. Labrador Retriever
2. Horse
3. Rabbit
4. Cat
5. Elephant
6. Octopus
7. Killer Whale
8. Puffin
9. Owl
10. Unicorn
11. Peacock
12. Mouse
13. Panda
14. Moose
15. Poodle
16. Polar Bear
17. Gorilla
18. Goldfish
19. Turkey
20. Pig
21. Ox
22. Lion
23. Hippogryph
24. Penguin
25. Kangaroos (mama and baby)
26. Monkey
27. Ram
28. Shark
29. Parrot
30. Raccoon
31. Ray
32. Rhino
33. Chicken
34. Tiger
35. Cheetah
36. Rooster
37. Deer with Antlers
38. Fox
39. Giraffe
40. Koala
41. Dolphin
42. Eagle
43. Sloth
44. Hippo
45. Duck
46. Dragon
47. Chameleon
48. Crocodile
49. Dinosaur (T. Rex in Jurassic Park)
50. Toucan

ISBN: 978-1522925781
by: Adult Coloring Book Sets
Copyrights © 2016 All rights reserved

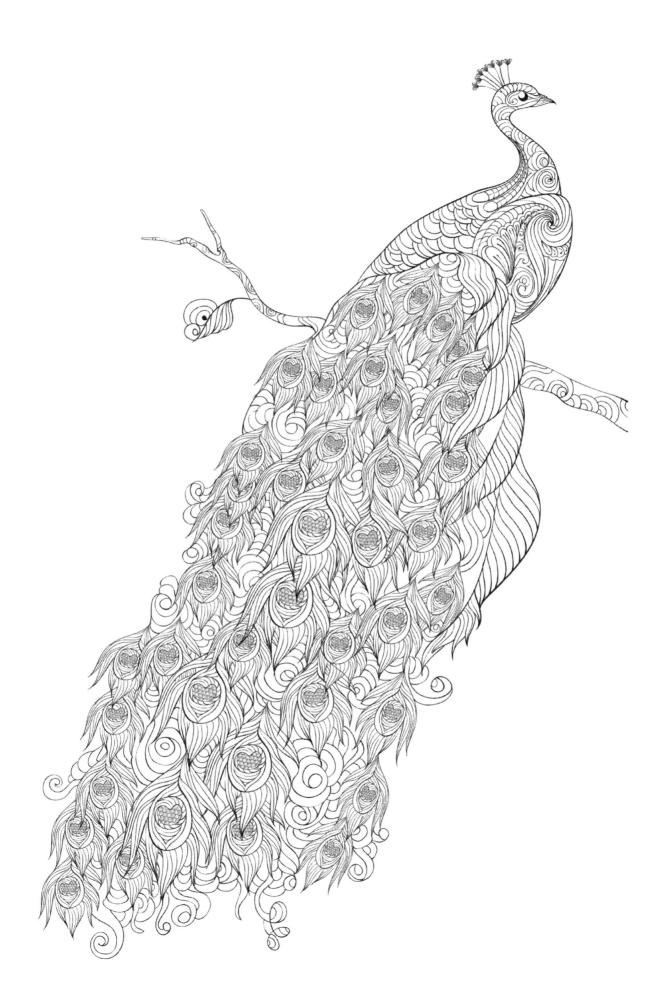

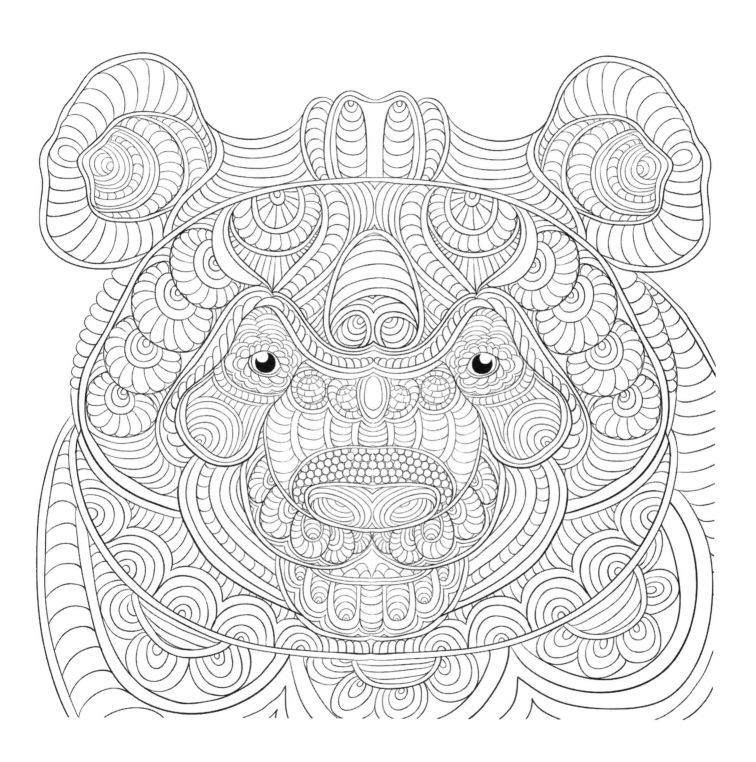

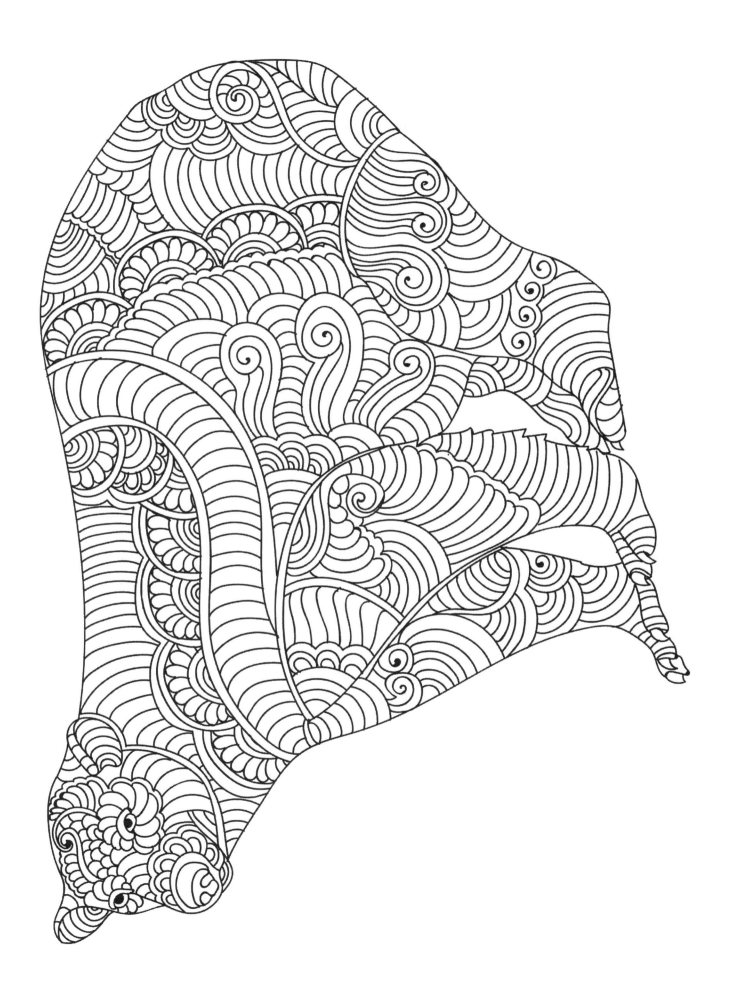

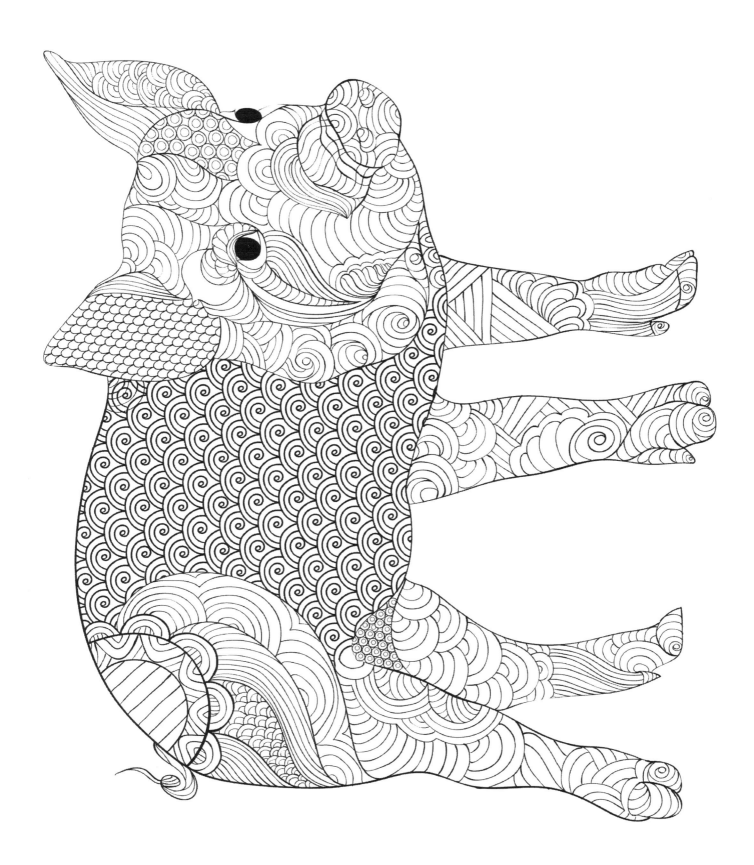

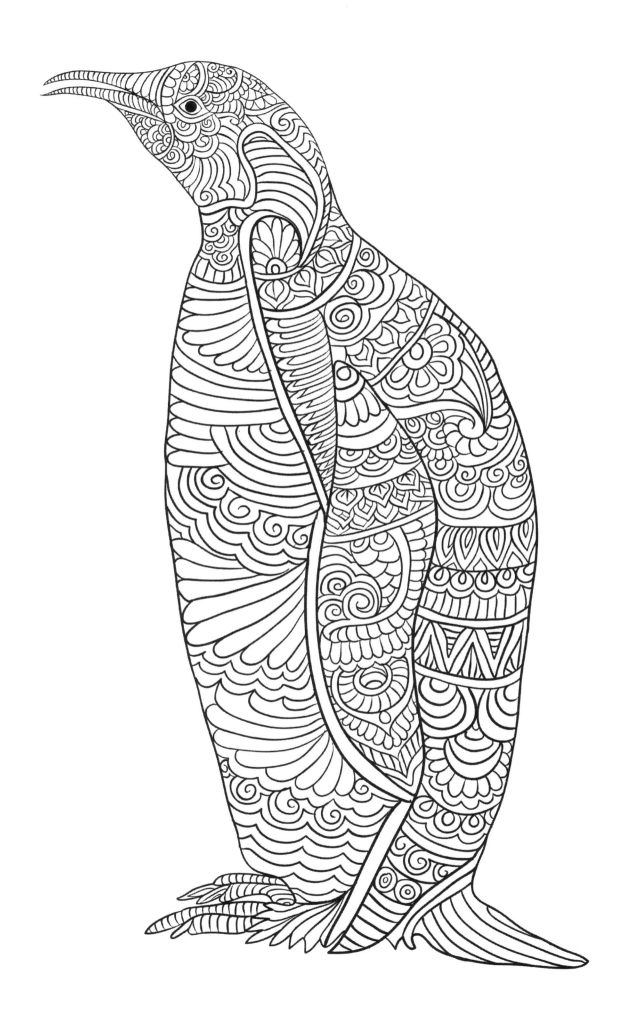

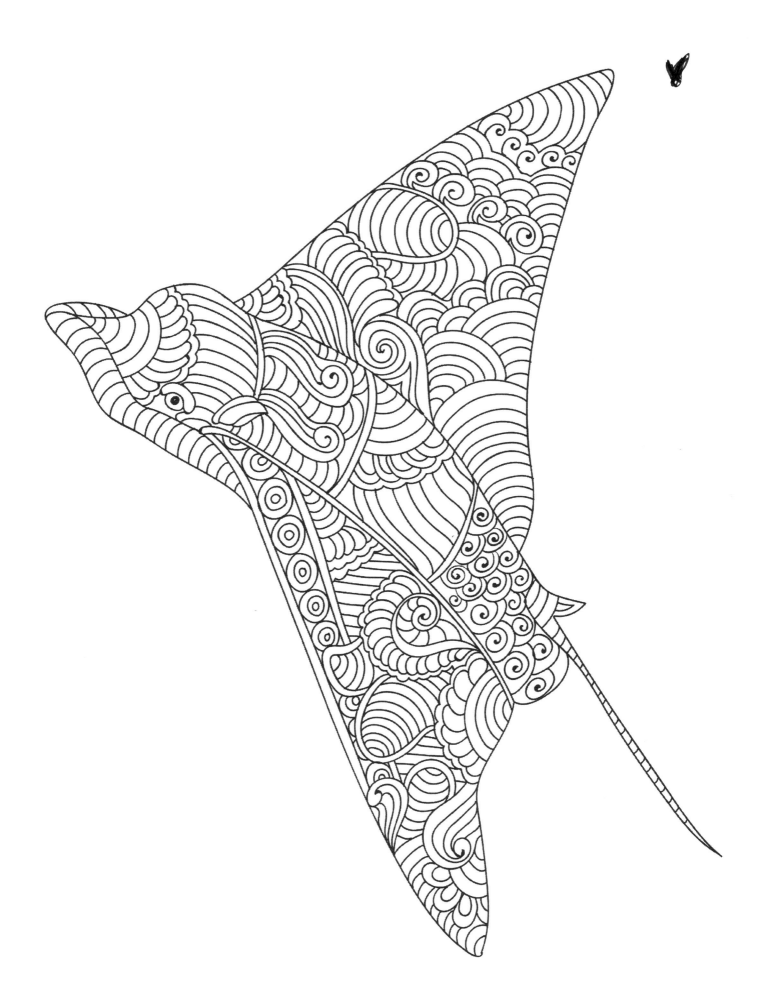

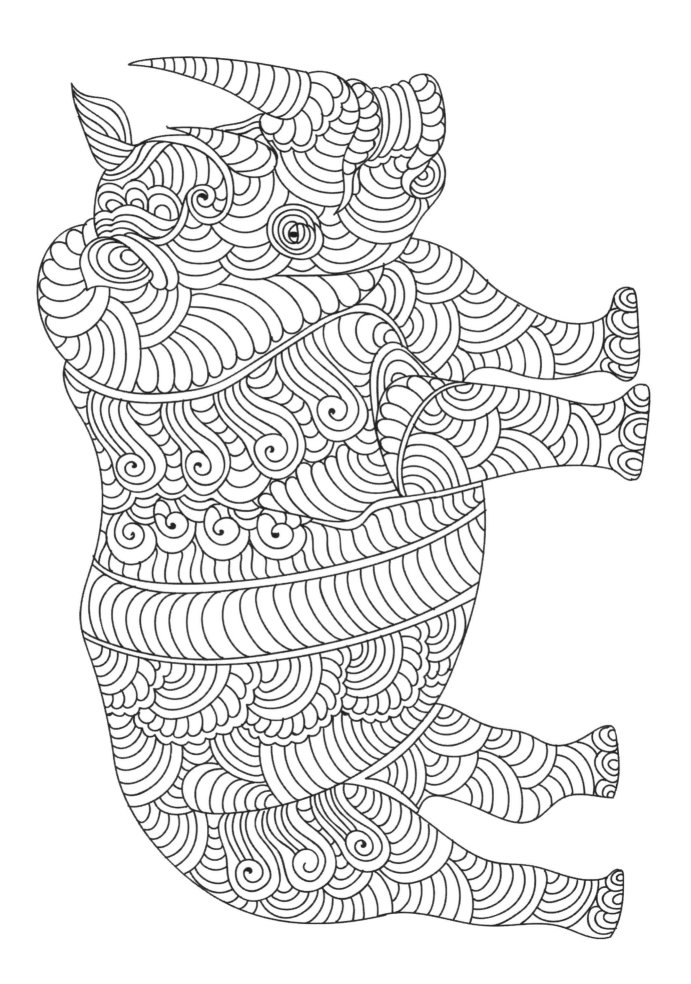

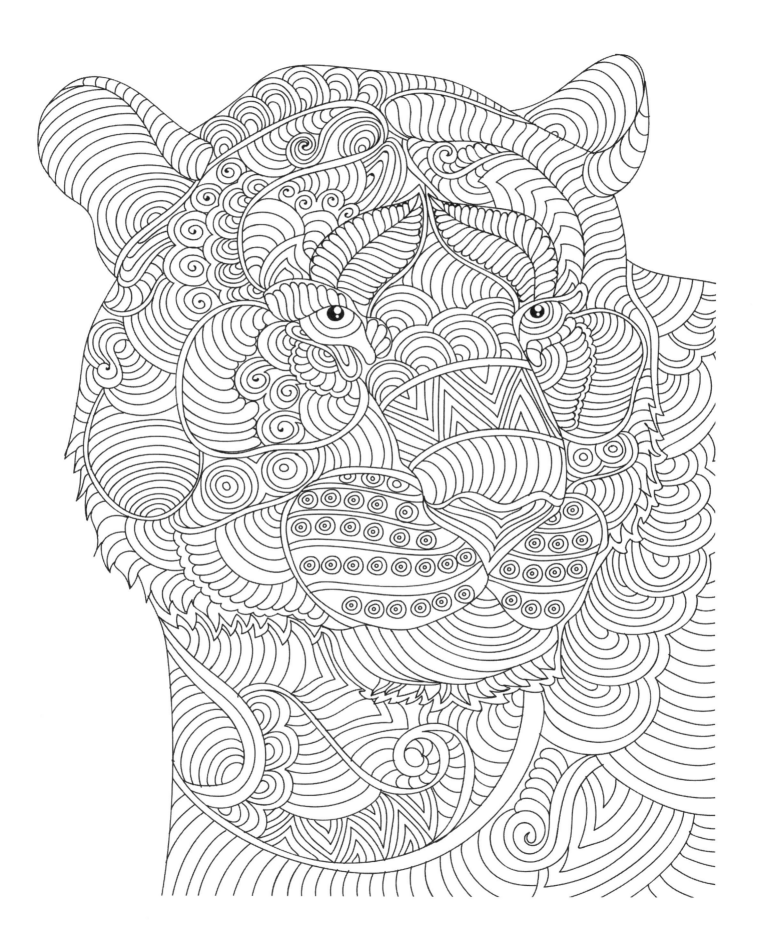

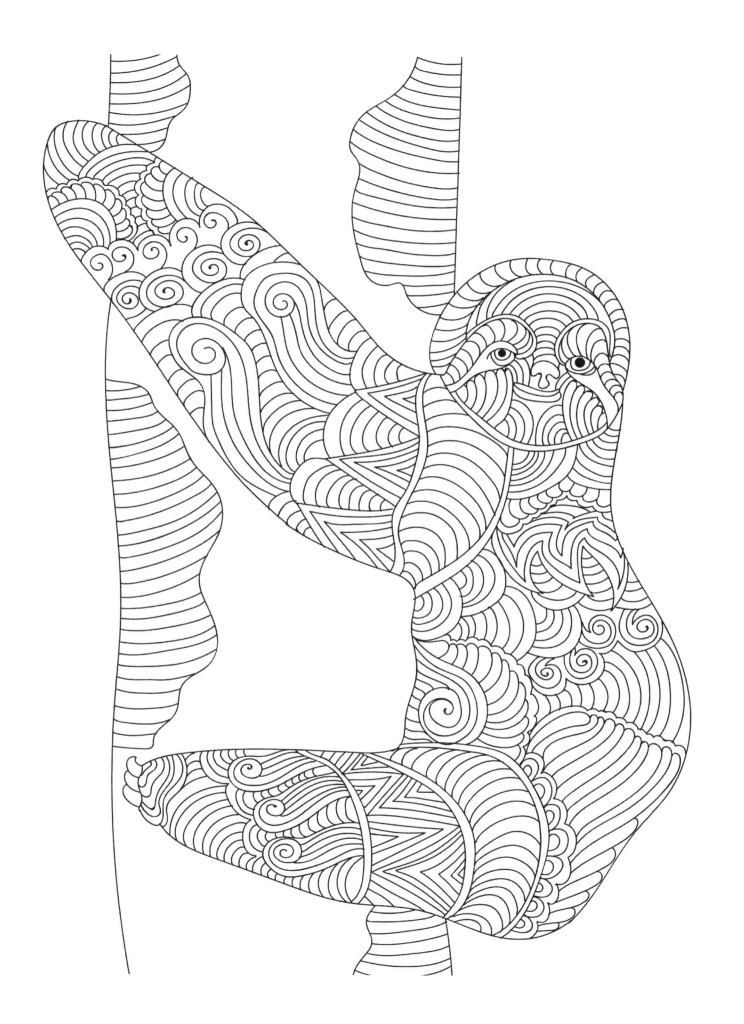

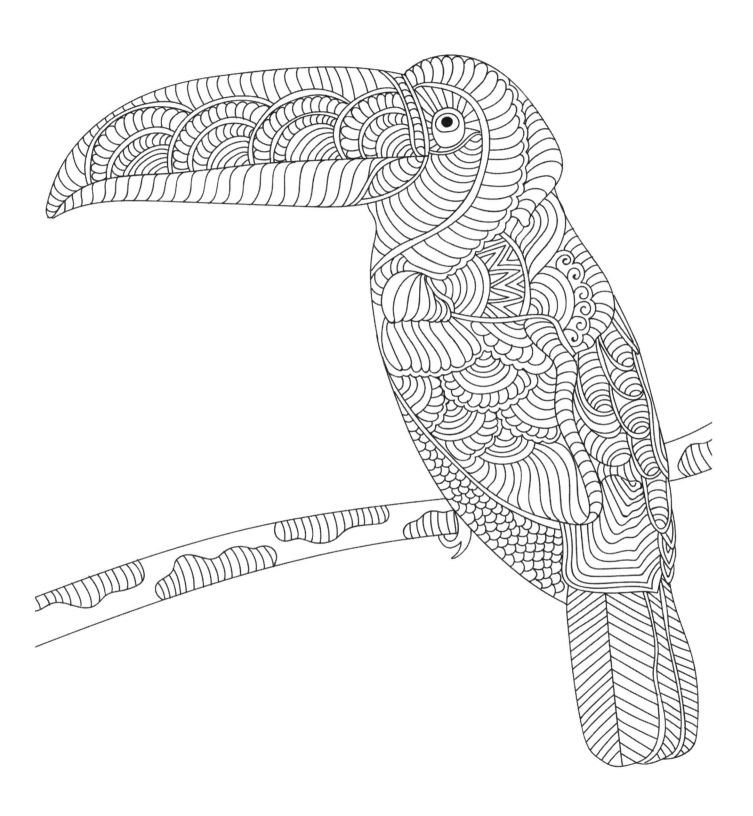

Free Bonus Book

$3.99 value electronic coloring book, easy to print out. Download your FREE book now:

http://CoolAdultColoringBooks.com

More: Check our website above for new books and special promotion deals…

Made in the USA
Charleston, SC
03 January 2016